IF YOU WERE . . .
A PHOTOGRAPHER

Carol Watson
Illustrated by Valeria Petrone

Belitha Press

With thanks to Chalky Whyte –
photographer

First published by Belitha Press Limited
31 Newington Green
London N16 9PU

ISBN 1 85561 065 5

Printed in Hong Kong by Imago

Introduction

Have you ever thought about what you would like to be when you grow up, leave school and go out to work? There are so many jobs to choose from, and they all need different talents, knowledge and skills.

Sometimes you might think you would like to be a doctor, a pilot, a ballet dancer, a teacher or a photographer . . . but you don't really know what your life would be like if you were actually in that job. You also don't know if your personality would be suited to the job, so that you would be able to enjoy it and do it well.

IF YOU WERE . . . is a series of bright, new information books through which you can learn about a particular job, by following the story of the main characters as they go about their work.

In this book, you can follow Liz Flick, a fashion photographer, as she goes off on a shoot – and discover that even the most glamorous jobs involve a lot of hard work.

At the back of the book there are some details about other kinds of photographers, how you can become a photographer, and the sort of person you need to be to enjoy the work.

It's Monday afternoon and Liz Flick's taxi draws up at the airport terminal. Liz is a photographer and she is on her way to a fashion shoot.

Rod, Liz's assistant, unloads the bags, cameras and other equipment.
"I hope the rest of the crew are here," he says to Liz.

They make their way to the check-in desk. Rod checks in the bags and boxes, but keeps the cameras with him as they are very fragile.

"Hi," says a voice. They look around, and see the rest of the team waiting nearby. Rod quickly counts them all to see everyone is there.

The fashion crew make their way to the departure lounge. As they do this they have to pass through the airport security check.

Rod has to open the boxes to show the officials the cameras inside. Everything has to go through the X-ray machine.

Later they hear an announcement. "Flight B13445 to Barbados now boarding at Gate 5." Liz and her crew board the aeroplane.

There's Josie, the make-up lady, three models, Louis, the hairdresser, Beth, the wardrobe lady and Serena, the fashion editor who is their client.

On the 'plane Liz chats to Serena about the fashion shots that are needed for her magazine. They discuss ideas and schedules for the next day.

Serena needs six pages of fashion photographs for her magazine. "We have a lot to do in two days," says Liz. "It'll be hard work for everyone."

At last they reach Barbados. This is their location, where the fashion shoot will take place.
"It looks beautiful," says Serena.

The sun is setting over the island as the 'plane comes into land. It's been a very long flight and they are all keen to reach the hotel.

After the plane has landed, the team claim their bags and boxes and go through customs. A mini-bus meets them to take the crew to the hotel.

Once all the luggage and equipment is loaded up, the crew pile into the bus and set off on the last stage of their journey.

"Well, here we are!" says Liz, as they draw up at the hotel. The porters help them to unload all their vital equipment.

Everyone is feeling tired and hungry. They are relieved to check into their rooms to freshen up and get ready for dinner.

Later over dinner, the fashion team chat to each other. Josie, Louis and Beth have all worked together before and talk about old times.

The models are very careful what they eat and drink. They have to watch their weight, and keep their skin looking good.

"I'm off to bed," says Liz, once the meal is over. "Remember, we've to be up at 5 a.m. tomorrow morning. You'll need all the sleep you can get!"

After their long journey everyone is ready for bed. They all say goodnight, and ask the hotel receptionist for early alarm calls.

At 5 a.m. the next morning, Liz's telephone rings. "Your alarm call, Ms Flick," a voice says. "Thanks," says Liz sleepily.

Although she is still tired, Liz forces herself to get up. She must be wide awake and ready to start the day's hard work.

Liz dresses hurriedly, and has a quick breakfast. She carefully checks through her detailed list of plans for the day ahead.

There is a knock on her door. "Ready?" asks Rod, who is waiting to check out the first location with Liz and Serena.

Liz and Rod meet up with Serena, and set off for the beach which is close to the hotel.
They look around carefully.

"We could do some shots over on the jetty," suggests Liz, and Serena agrees. Rod goes off to make sure the jetty is safe.

Meanwhile in another hotel room Josie, Louis and Beth have been up since 5 a.m. preparing the model's hair, make-up and clothes.

Grace's hair has been washed, dried and plaited, but Mona's long blonde hair is going to look wild and loose for the beach.

Rick's short, cropped hair does not need much fuss, but he has to have a smooth shave, so his chin does not look dark and bristly.

The models dress in their swimsuits. Serena needs photographs of beachwear for the summer edition of her magazine.

At 6.30 a.m. the fashion team meet in the hotel foyer.
"Are we all ready?" asks Liz.
Rick is still looking very sleepy.

Rod does a head count and they all set off for the beach. Everyone helps to carry the bags and equipment needed for the shoot.

At the beach Rod sets up the tripod and camera, and uses the light meter to check that the light is good enough to take photographs.

Josie and Louis hold the reflectors which reflect the sun's light and make everything brighter. Liz needs as much light as possible for good shots.

"Can you pose by the sea, Grace?" Liz asks. She wants to take some quick Polaroid photographs, which develop instantly in the camera.

Liz shows the Polaroid photographs to Serena to give her a rough idea of what further final photographs might look like.

Rick and Mona pose by the jetty, while Liz takes more Polaroids of this different setting. Again she and Serena look at the result.

"Looks wonderful," says Serena. "That old fishing boat could be good, too," Liz suggests. Rod goes off to talk to the fisherman on the boat.

Rod asks the fisherman if they can use his boat for the shoot. The fisherman is pleased as Rod pays him money to use the boat.

"Mona, can we try you on the boat?" asks Liz. Mona climbs nervously on to the fishing boat while the fisherman sits happily smiling beside her.

"That's terrific!" says Liz, snapping a polaroid for Serena to see.
"OK, Rod, load up the film, we're ready to shoot."

Once the lighting and equipment is ready, Mona poses while Liz takes photographs from different angles. Some are close-ups, others long shots.

Liz has to change the lens on her camera when she does close-ups. She has lots of different lenses, and spare cameras in case one goes wrong.

"Right, we'll try some shots on the jetty!" calls Liz.
"Can we have Rick and Grace together here, please."

Rick and Grace run along the jetty towards Liz, who is quickly snapping as many shots as she can as they move.

Liz takes lots of photographs. She needs to do this as only some of the shots will be in focus, because the models are moving.

Grace changes and Liz takes close-ups of Grace on her own in different outfits.
"Looks good, Grace!" she says.

"Turn to the left – smile. That's good!" says Liz.
"Now toss your head back and laugh. Great!"

The crew take a break for lunch. Serena and Liz talk over the morning's work, and plan more shots for the afternoon.

After their break, the models change again. Josie and Louis fix their hair and make-up, while Beth looks after the clothes.

The crew work again all afternoon, until Liz and Serena think they have enough shots. By now they are all feeling very tired.

"OK, that's it," says Liz finally. Rod packs up the cameras and equipment. The others gather up the bags and everyone heads for the hotel.

Now the crew can relax. They have a drink together and a quick dip in the hotel pool, before dinner. It's been a long, hard day.

"It's another early rise, tomorrow," says Liz. "The mini-bus will pick us up at 6.30 a.m. Get as much sleep as you can."

The next day's shoot is in a different location. This time the crew are in the colourful, leafy grounds of a grand old house.

Serena wants beautiful pictures of summer dresses and evening wear, and Rick will model the latest in men's fashions.

Rod and Liz talk over the arrangements with the owner of the house. The crew have rented the gardens just for the day.

"I hope the weather is going to hold," says Serena. "The sky doesn't look good." Liz is worried about the lack of light, too.

The crew begin the first shoot. Rick, Mona and Grace pose together amongst the exotic plants and flowers in the garden.

Rod and Liz use the reflectors again, and Liz also stands on a stepladder to get extra height and a different angle on the scene.

"The light is getting worse," says Liz. Sure enough the sun has disappeared. Large, threatening black clouds are gathering above them.

Suddenly, a gigantic flash of lightning shoots across the sky, and there is a loud clap of thunder. The rain pours down in torrents. "Oh no!" Rod grabs the equipment and the crew run for cover. They head for the house, not far away. The owner opens the door to let them in.

Josie looks in horror as the make-up runs down the model's faces.

Louis moans at the state of their hair. "We'll have to start again," says Liz.

Liz and Serena look around the old house. There is grand staircase and some large elegant rooms. "We could shoot here," says Liz.

They talk once again to the owner and offer to pay him for the use of his house. He is very happy for them to film in his home.

Louis starts work on Mona's hair. "It took me ages to get this right this morning," he says. "I hope I can do it again!"

Meanwhile, Josie re-does both Grace's and Rick's make-up. She works quickly as they have a lot of photographs to get through that day.

Then Beth and Serena sort out fresh dry, clothes for the models to wear. "I think we'll have evening dress, next," suggests Serena.

The models change and prepare for the next session. Beth pins up a hem, which has fallen down on Grace's dress.

As they are filming inside, Rod sets up some powerful lights. These have little silver umbrellas attached to them which help reflect the light.

When everything and everyone is ready Liz starts off the session. The models look stunning and Serena is very pleased with how things look.

"Now we'll have some individual shots," says Liz. She takes close-ups of each model on their own, showing the details of the clothes they wear.

"Let's move into the drawing room," suggests Serena. Rod sets up the equipment and Liz and Serena re-arrange the furniture.

Grace poses by the grand piano. She is very elegant and her dress looks beautiful. "Terrific!" says Liz snapping away.

Mona's long, blonde hair has been swept up away from her face in a graceful style that suits her. "Wonderful!" calls Liz.

At last the shoot is over. Liz has taken more photographs than they need so there are lots to choose from. They will only use the best for the magazine.

They load up the mini-bus and set off once again for the hotel. The rain has stopped now, and the crew take a last look at the sights of the island.

Next morning it's time to leave for home. There is no time to relax and lie in the sun, as Liz has lots to do once she's back.

"Goodbye, Barbados," says Josie as the 'plane shoots up into the sky. "Perhaps I'll come back for a holiday, one day," she thinks.

The next day, back home, Liz is working hard again developing the black-and-white photographs she took on the shoot.

Liz has her own dark room for this. There is no light except for a special orange bulb so that she can see what she is doing.

Liz takes the rolls of colour film to a laboratory to be developed.

When they are ready she collects all the transparencies.

A few days later Liz meets with Serena and the art director of the magazine. She shows them all the photographs which have worked well.

"I think there's a good selection here for you to choose from," says Liz. "There's a fantastic shot of Grace on the jetty!"

They put the colour transparencies on a light box, and look at them through a special magnifying glass, so they can see them in detail.

The black-and-white photographs are displayed on a contact sheet as the negatives are difficult to see. Serena and the art director study them closely.

Together they decide which photographs they like best and Serena and the art director choose the ones they will use for the magazine.

"You've done a great job, Liz," says Serena. "The summer issue of the magazine will look good!" Liz's job is over now, and she says goodbye.

Once the vital photographs have been chosen, the designer works out how they are to appear on the inside pages and cover of the magazine.

Serena writes the information she wants to go with the photographs. Then the transparencies and the layout is sent off to be processed.

A few days later the proofs of the layout arrive. Serena and the art director study the shots. Mona looks stunning on the cover.

At last the magazine is out on sale! Liz leafs through the pages to see how it looks. "Well," she says. "The hard work was worth it, after all!"

FACTS ABOUT BEING A PHOTOGRAPHER

There are many different kinds of photographer. These include:

A Social Photographer

This is someone who takes photographs of weddings, local events and does family portraits. To be this kind of photographer you need to be friendly and like people. You should be imaginative, quick-thinking, very patient, and have a strong voice, so that people can hear your instructions!

A Press Photographer

Press photographers work for newspapers or magazines. The work involves taking photographs for news features or stories written by a reporter or journalist. Sometimes this means photographing dramas such as fires, accidents, earthquakes or even wars; but more often it involves local events, such as entertainments, exhibitions or celebrations.

These kind of photographers need to think and act quickly, be good with people and like travelling. They have to be able to write and spell facts correctly and be happy to work at any time – days, nights and weekends.

A Medical Photographer

This is someone who takes photographs in hospitals or medical schools. Most of the work involves photographing patients with diseases or ailments to help the doctors and students to learn more about how to help people. To do this work, the photographer needs to be able to deal with frightened people who are seriously ill, have special medical knowledge, and be able to use complicated hospital equipment.

An Advertising or Fashion Photographer

This is the most popular kind of photography, and the most difficult area to get into. These kind of photographers are employed by magazines, advertising agencies and large companies. They take photographs of models wearing the latest fashions, or of actors advertising products. People think that this kind of photography is the most exciting and glamorous, but very few photographers succeed and the work is hard.

To be this kind of photographer you need to be tough, confident, artistic, be able to organise and control a team of people, like travelling, enjoy a great deal of responsibility and be able to take the blame if something goes wrong. These photographers have deadlines to meet and need to work long hours under pressure.

Other kinds of photographers are: **Police Photographers, Industrial Photographers, Editorial Photographers and Scientific Photographers.**

All photographers need to be hardworking and enthusiastic because most of the work is not well-paid, and therefore it is important to do the job because you enjoy it.

If you want to be a photographer

1. Most photographers learn the job by becoming an assistant to someone who is already a successful professional. This person then teaches them all the skills and qualifications 'on the job'.

2. Some people learn about photography by taking a course at a Technical College or a College of Art and Design. First you have to know what kind of photographer you want to be, and then choose the most suitable course.